Why Suffering?

Paul W. Nisly

HERALD PRESS
Scottdale, Pennsylvania
Kitchener, Ontario

The Visitation Pamphlets are directed to specific personal needs. They are designed to be given by pastors, chaplains, doctors, nurses, and all who would share at an appropriate moment words of hope and faith.

Blessings by Your Bedside by John M. Drescher
By Still Waters by John M. Drescher
Empty Arms by Mary Joyce Rae and Robert W. Rae
Facing Illness with Faith by John M. Drescher
For the Golden Years by John M. Drescher
For Hospital Days by Robert W. Rae
Grief's Slow Work by Harold Bauman
I Lift My Eyes by John M. Drescher
In Grief's Lone Hour by John M. Drescher
Just in for Tests by Robert Rae
May Your Marriage Be a Happy One by John M. Drescher
Personal Prescriptions by John M. Drescher
Shut In But Not Shut Out by Mary Joyce Rae
Sources of Spiritual Strength by John M. Drescher
Spiritual Nutrients by John M. Drescher
Strength for Suffering by John M. Drescher
Suffering and God's Presence by John M. Drescher
To the New Mother by Helen Good Brenneman
What Can I Say? by Robert W. Rae
Why Suffering? by Paul W. Nisly

WHY SUFFERING?
Copyright © 1980 by Herald Press, Scottdale, Pa. 15683
   Published simultaneously in Canada by Herald Press,
   Kitchener, Ont. N2G 4M5
International Standard Book Number: 0-8361-1914-2
Printed in the United States of America
Design: Alice B. Shetler/Cover Photo: Paul M. Schrock

15 14 13 12 11 10 9 8 7 6 5 4 3 2 1

Preface

Suffering is almost as old as the human race. Most people throughout history have simply assumed that suffering is part of the human experience. But today some well-meaning Christians tell us that suffering is fundamentally unnecessary, that suffering is the direct result of sin, an evidence of a lack of proper faith, and that God will bring healing if His conditions are met.

In our experience, however, not all faithful Christians are healed, not all suffering alleviated. If you are suffering, being told that you need not suffer is not much comfort. Although the mystery of suffering cannot be fully explained, we can trust the God who created us to care for us. God is with us in our difficulties even though He may not remove the hard circumstances.

Many people have contributed to my understanding of suffering, and thus to the writing of this booklet. I wish to mention particularly my wife, Laura, who has lived courageously with rheumatoid arthritis for over nine years, and my mother, who taught me much from the confines of her bed and chair.

Paul W. Nisly
Grantham, Pennsylvania.

Why Suffering?

A few days ago a good friend, a fun-loving college senior, came to my office in considerable distress. He is a young man with great wit, one who keeps classes lively with his cleverness and insight, but on the day of his visit he was unexpectedly solemn. "Much of my laughter," he told me, "is a mask to hide the pain I'm experiencing."

In our long conversation he told me about his mother whose limbs are gradually becoming paralyzed and whose illness, her doctors now say, is probably terminal. In his anguish he said, "I think I could bear the suffering for myself, but I can't understand God's 'doing' this to my mother. I have been careless and I probably deserve to be punished—but my mother is the most godly person I know."

Compounding the doubt and confusion in my

friend's mind is his father's attitude toward the situation. His father is sure that his wife will be healed. In fact, according to my friend, his father believes one must simply claim healing as an accomplished fact—and God will respond. Yet the woman's physical condition is progressively deteriorating.

My friend is confronting the old problem of human suffering, but no longer is the problem abstract, a philosophical question. He is personally and experientially involved in the dilemma: If God is good—and all-powerful—why is there so much suffering in the world? Can one believe in a compassionate God? And how does the human spirit in distress experience God's mercy? Does suffering have any meaning, or is it the result of an uncaring universe? In short, why suffering?

Do Christians Suffer?

The question, you may say, is silly. Haven't you just been describing the suffering of a Christian? But not all would agree that suffering is a part of life. Most radical are those who deny the physical reality of suffering. If one dismisses error through thinking truth—so the argument goes—there is no pain. Most of us probably would not accept this position because it sets up a radical and unscriptural dualism between flesh and spirit.

More persuasive are those who argue for the power of thinking positively. And we would acknowledge that many illnesses are psychosomatic, which is to say that they have their origin primarily in the mental rather than the physical process. But the faulty assumption of this position—at least in its extreme expression—is that all physical ailments are caused by mental problems.

Finally, there are Christians who, like my friend's father, fervently believe in God's healing for all. Thus suffering is viewed as being unnecessary for the faithful Christian. On one occasion I heard a preacher rather ironically announce that if we really thought suffering was so great, we should all come, kneel at the altar, and pray that we might experience it, the implication being that only fools or nonbelievers would be ill or experiencing suffering. Yet our experience would not seem to support this position. And both Old and New Testaments record numerous instances of suffering.

What Is the Source of Suffering?

Recently I heard a Bible teacher argue that human suffering is either a result of God's chastening hand, in which case we need to repent, or the devil is trying to "lay one on us," in which case we need to rebuke him and the suffering he has brought. A similar view was expressed by a visitor to a hospitalized friend of mine when he asked my friend, "Is this sickness from God or the devil?" His question no doubt grew from his perception that sickness and suffering are the result of sin. Now we must acknowledge that sin does often bring suffering. Alcoholism, for example, often leads to cirrhosis of the liver and a host of other physical and social problems.

While we do not know much about the background of the paralytic man whom Jesus healed, we hear Jesus say, "See, you are well again. Stop sinning or something worse may happen to you" (John 5:14). Personal sin can—and often does—cause suffering. And in an ultimate sense sin brought suffering to the human race.

But we should not believe that because a specific person suffers he or she is necessarily personally guilty. Such an attitude is grossly unfair and piles unwarranted guilt feelings on the recipient. Much suffering is simply a result of our finiteness, our creatureliness. We are, says the Apostle Paul, common clay pots (2 Corinthians 4:7). As mortal beings we are limited. We are not gods; we are created beings dependent upon God.

We suffer, but "why" often remains a mystery. In the account of Jesus' healing a man blind from birth, the disciples asked, "Who sinned, this man or his parents, that he was born blind?" (John 9:2). It was a common question. Jesus' contemporaries thought suffering was necessarily a sign of having fallen from God's favor. We hear similar questions today—and they may lead to self-condemnation for the sufferer.

But Jesus says, "Neither this man nor his parents sinned ... but this happened so that the work of God might be displayed in his life" (John 9:3). Can we bear this answer—that suffering may be to glorify God?

What Is the Meaning of Suffering?

In his profound little book *Does My Father Know I'm Hurt?* David Seel, a medical doctor in Korea, writes, "I must confess that the catalog of misery which walks before me at Tumor Clinic appalls me even after ten years of cancer work. *Is there no end* to the charade of life and the parade of death?" Yet, says Dr. Seel, "I cannot feel regret for having been involved in this uneven contest. It has taught me a profound admiration for contestants whose victories were not always in surviving, but rather, in how they failed" (p. 65, italics added).

"Is there no end?" The question continues ringing in one's mind. And as I listened to my student friend—listened more than spoke—I was forced to focus again my personal confrontation with the question of suffering.

My mother—also a God-fearing woman—was an invalid or semi-invalid for over seventeen years before her death. The list of her ailments was long: heart disease, severe kidney stone attacks, Parkinson's disease and, in late life, diabetes and possible stomach cancer. More questions than answers dominated my adolescent years at home.

The questions did not fade away with adulthood—though they receded for a time. In 1971 my wife began experiencing severe pain, pain which moved from one area of the body to another. There seemed to be no discernible pattern, and there was no quick diagnosis. On one occasion the pain—which was finally successfully diagnosed as rheumatoid arthritis—was so severe that she was unable to move from living room to bedroom without aid.

A young couple, husband in graduate school, two preschool children, *why us?*

Why Us?

Through the years we heard many statements—some helpful, some painful. By way of summary and critique I list the most common of those ideas:

1. *Assertion:* Sickness and suffering are a result of sin.

Response: This statement was sometimes implied, at other times made openly. It always hurt! We believe suffering *may* be a result of sin; often it is a consequence of our finiteness.

2. *Assertion:* God is a loving Father; therefore, we need not suffer.

Response: God *does* love us, but that fact does not remove us from our humanness. And sometimes believing that God loves us, while at the same time experiencing pain, leads to even greater anguish, especially when one cannot see an end to the situation.

3. *Assertion:* God is the great Healer; it is not His will that any should be ill.

Response: Repeatedly we have heard this statement. And we wondered, "What is wrong with *us* that healing doesn't take place?" Maybe *sin* is the issue after all. Finally, though, we have come to see that while God is both Creator and Sustainer, there is no assurance of immediate physical healing. God is sovereign and will not be manipulated.

4. *Assertion:* Healing is dependent on your faith; if you believe deeply enough, you will be healed.

Response: This position is, finally, unanswerable. It is the statement to end all discussion. And one begins to doubt: Are we—am I—even Christian? We are learning, though, that faith is our response to the faithfulness of God. It is not faith which heals; *God* is the Healer. And healing takes many forms.

Jesus cried, "Father, if you are willing, take this cup from me" (Luke 22:42). Would anyone accuse Him of unbelief? Yet the "cup" was not removed.

How Then Respond?

How, then, ought we respond to suffering? Victor Frankl, a Swiss psychiatrist who spent years in a German concentration camp, says that while we may not be able to change the *fact* of suffering, we are free to *choose our attitude* toward suffering.

The last human freedom, he says, is the freedom to choose our response to any given circumstance. In the concentration camp, for example, there were a few people who would walk through the camp, comforting others and giving away their own meager supply of bread. It was possible to transcend almost unbelievably bad circumstances.

While we cannot know perfectly the meaning of suffering, we can make the following affirmations:

(1) suffering reminds us of our finiteness, our limitedness;

(2) suffering pushes us to dependency upon God;

(3) suffering reminds us that life on earth is not forever.

Though never desired, never sought, physical suffering may give us that larger perspective which we would not otherwise have discovered. My wife and I have found this enrichment of meaning to be true in our lives—not easily nor all the time—but ultimately.